# Power In His Wings

## How the Prayer Closet misrepresents the Tallit

Dr. Christiaan J. de Ruiter

**Ruach Hakodesh publishing**

# Power in His Wings
## Study on the Tallit

**Eagle Wings Charismatic Ministries International**
**8100 Ingrid Drive, Elgin, Texas 78621**
www.ewcmi.us

**ISBN-13 : 978-0615570891**
**ISBN-10 : 0615570895**

**Printed in the United States of America**
© 2011, Dr. Christiaan J. de Ruiter / Eagle Wings Charismatic Ministries International

**All Scripture references are taken from**
**The Holy Bible King James Version**

No part of this publication may be reproduced, stored in or introduced into a retrieval system, or transmitted, in any form or by any means (electronic, mechanical, photocopying, recording or otherwise), without the prior written permission of the copyright owner.

# DEDICATION

This book is dedicated to all the members of Eagle Wings Charismatic Ministries International and their Berean Search of the truth as provided in the Holy Word of God almighty, the Bible.

# CONTENTS

|   | Acknowledgments | i |
|---|---|---|
| 1 | Introduction | 1 |
| 2 | A special garment | 5 |
| 3 | Background of the Tallit | 11 |
| 4 | Gematria of the Tallit | 15 |
| 5 | Wearing the Tallit | 21 |
| 6 | Tallit Scriptures | 29 |
| 7 | How to wear the Tallit | 31 |
| 8 | Religiosity of the Tallit | 33 |

### Appendices

| A | Scriptures and Key words | 35 |
|---|---|---|
| B | Hebrew - English | 41 |
| C | Strongs References | 43 |
|   | About the Author | 45 |

# ACKNOWLEDGMENTS

This bible study book is a compilation of the Sermon notes of Pastor Christiaan J. de Ruiter with additional information from the Shofarman, Elisabeth Syre, Dr. John Louis Muratori, and Rabi Milgrom.
Thiswas previously available as
"The Tallit, Why, How, When".
My gratitude goes out to my wife Wilma, who always gave me a nudge to continue when I needed it most.
Sister Lenita Reed, whom has patiently kept an eye out on the quality of this publication, and whose editing skills I could not do without.
To Dr. Jeffery Davidson who always has been a wonderful friend and a great motivator.
Last but not least to the Holy Spirit Provided to us by Jesus Christ as "the comforter" and vessel between us and the word of our Lord and Savior giving us access to the Rhema word of God.

# 1 INTRODUCTION

There is a new revival going on which involves a hard core study of the roots of our faith, placing emphasis on the truth of the original language (Hebrew and Greek).

In this revival, old walls are broken down and replacement theology or supersessionism is being destroyed. Replacement theology is nothing new, for centuries the Jewish customs and traditions have been removed from Christianity. Many misguided leaders have stated that the Christian church is the replacement for the chosen people the Jews. With this we have removed important information from the Bible, namely the understanding of the Word of God, the way that Jesus read it. Translations have been made to give better understanding which in reality took away from the truth of the word. We have been robbed of the depth of understanding of the roots of our faith due to persecutions over centuries against true believers and Jews alike.

Around AD 313 Constantine officiated Christianity as the official religion which led to no more persecution of the Christian believers.

AD 315 Anti Semitic sentiment was brought into Anti Semitic law "it is a crime for Jews to proselytize".

Around 320-340 AD following emperor Constantine changed views, a lot of his opinions, politics, and theology became slowly but surely doctrine. This is how his hatred against everything Jewish started the replacement theology, or supersessionism.


AD 325 to 1434 the church began building up a legal regime thus removing the Jews from Christian Society.

In the Council of Nicaea (325), Constantine ordained that the date of the Christian Easter should no longer be linked to that of the Jewish Passover, declaring, *"It is unbecoming that on the holiest of festivals we should follow the customs of the Jews; hencefort let us have nothing in common with that odious people."*

In Synod of Clermont (535), Jews were prohibited from holding public office.

In Synod of Orleans (538), Jews were barred from owning Christian slaves or employing Christian Servants.

In Synod of Gerona (1078), Jews were obligated to pay taxes for support of the church to the same extent as the Christians.

In the Third Lateran Council (1179), Jews are prohibited from suing or being witnesses against Christians in courts.

In the Fourth Lateran Council (1215), Jews are required to wear distinctive dress (eventually implemented by means of a yellow badge).

In the Council of Oxford (1222), construction of new synagogues is prohibited.

In the Synod of Breslau (1267), Jews are forced to reside in ghettos.

In the Synod of Ofen (1279), Christians are prohibited from selling or renting real estate to Jews.

During the Council of Basel (1434), Jews are barred from obtaining academic degrees.

Some of the most Anti-Semitic writings in history came out of Martin Luther's pen. "The Jews and Their Lies" was a program by Luther on how to deal with the Jews. The Reformation was a missed opportunity. Martin Luther and his 95 Theses shattered the Catholic Church's monopoly on Christian Theology. Instead of rejecting, Martin Luther embraced Replacement Theology.

By the end of 1800's to the start of the 1900's, a Holy Spirit Revival started with the Azusa Street Revival.

In 1906, there was the start of Holy Spirit Filled Churches Pentecostal, Four Square, and Apostolic.

In the 1960's, there was a Charismatic movement that was fired up by the Holy Spirit resulting in the birth of Charismatic churches.

The Hippie Movement started the Jesus Freaks. Scores of people started unorganized Bible Studies and questions about the church establishment.

The 20th century brought about the rise of the Silent Christian Majority support for Israel.

In 2004, Christians United for Israel.

All these activities prompted more awareness, more people, Lay and Clergy starting to study Hebrew and Greek.

The realization that a lot of changes by the Church has moved us away from Christ and our Jewish brothers and sisters.

Christiaan J. de Ruiter

> We are crafted into the branch,
> we have not replaced it.

We have been robbed of much depth of the understanding of the roots of our faith due to persecutions over centuries against true believers and Jews alike.

## 2 A SPECIAL GARMENT

The new testament tells us about a woman with a really strong faith. We do not know her name and neither do we know where she came from. What we do know is that she knew the prophets and that she understood the words of the prophet Malachi as written in Chapter 4 verse 2.

This woman was seriously ill and maybe even desperate. Matthew, Mark and Luke wrote about this woman of faith.

*Matthew 9:20-22 "And, behold, a woman, which was diseased with an issue of blood twelve years, came behind him, and touched the hem of his garment: For she said within herself, If I may but touch his garment, I shall be whole. But Jesus turned him about, and when he saw her, he said, Daughter, be of good comfort; thy faith hath made thee whole. And the woman was made whole from that hour."*

*Mark 5:24-26 "And Jesus went with him; and much people followed him, and thronged him. And a certain woman, which had an issue of blood twelve years, and had suffered many things of many physicians, and had spent all that she had, and was nothing bettered, but rather grew worse,"*

*Luke 8:43-46 "And a woman having an issue of blood twelve years, which had spent all her living upon physicians, neither could be healed of any, Came behind him, and touched the border of his garment: and immediately her issue of blood stanched. And Jesus said, Who touched me? When all denied, Peter and they that were with him said, Master, the multitude throng thee and press thee, and sayest thou, Who touched me? And Jesus said, Somebody hath touched me: for I perceive that virtue is gone out of me."*

When we put on our investigator's hat, we take these witness testimonies apart and then glue them back together in a more or less time constructed sequence that shows the whole picture in a very clear way.

[MK] And Jesus went with him; and many people followed him, and thronged him. [L] A woman having an issue of blood twelve years had spent all her living on physicians. She neither could be healed of any, [MK] and had suffered many things of many physicians, and had spent all that she had, and was nothing bettered, but rather grew worse. [MW] She said within herself, "If I may but touch his garment, I shall be whole." [L] She came behind him and touched the border of his garment: and immediately her issue of blood stanched. [L] Jesus then said, "Who touched me?" When all denied, Peter and they that were with him said,

"Master, the multitude throng you and press you, and say you, Who touched me?" [MW] But Jesus turned him about, and when he saw her, he said, "Daughter, be of good comfort; your faith has made you whole. And the woman was made whole from that hour."
[MW] Matthew [MK] Mark [L] Luke

When we read the eye witness stories in this way, we are getting a very clear picture on what was going on at the moment. A throng of people, and one woman pushing through in faith, reaching down in the eye of the danger of being trampled.

This woman's faith had healed her: the faith in the prophets of old and the truth in the words of the scripture given by the Heavenly Father.

However, the question for us is, what was it that this woman touched and what was it that she knew in faith that would heal her from her illness. She had been bleeding for twelve years and none of the doctors could help her. What was it that she knew would make this prophet, this Jesus of Nazareth, different from any of the quacks she has been to? She touched the border of His garment, but it was not just the border or hem of any garment; she touched was His tallit.

When we look at the text more closely, we realize that the woman touched the fringe of the tallit, the prayer-shawl, the corner fringes we call the tzitzit.

*Malachi 4:2 reads "But to you that fear my name shall the Sun of righteousness arise with healing in his wings; and you shall go forth, and grow up as calves of the stall."*

But to you who believe in me YaWeH, my son Jesus Christ the Messiah Yeshua Ha'meshiach shall appear and He will have healing in His fringes, the tzitzit. And you who shall realize this shall jump out as calves who have let out of the stall.

Within the ages, as we have read in chapter one, people have done their best to remove the references of Judaism and the Jews out of the Holy Bible. This story again is one of those prime examples: take out that strange garment that those Jews are wearing and call it the hem of His garment. With that, more was removed then just a Jewish reference. The words of the prophet Malachi were also watered down.

The tallit holds a great importance for Jews and Christians alike. It is a garment given by God to His people.

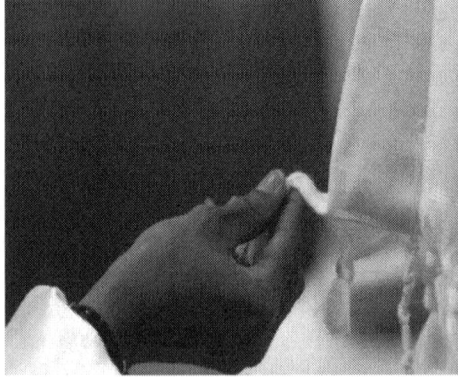

It is not that this garment has special healing power, but the faith in Jehovah Rapha, God our Healer, Jesus Christ, the great physician does. It is the understanding of the healing as written in Malachi 4:2 and moving in faith, forgetting about the consequences, the risks and dangers. The bending, going down deep, to where there is no other direction anymore then up. That kind of faith, the complete surrender, is what brings the healing. Understanding how God works and how we need to be relying on Him and Him alone, brings the healing. When we are in addiction, so deep down that we are on our backs and there is only one way out- UP! That is when we see the hand stretched out to us, and that is when we can and will receive that handshake of salvation: that handshake of healing.

The woman knew the important words of the prophet of old that there would be healing for her in His tzitzit. That is why she went down to that prophet, with the healing power, and felt that If she only touch the tzitzit on His tallit, then she would be healed.

How did she know, because the word of God told her so, through His prophet Malachi.

And as written in *psalm 57:1 "Be merciful to me, O God, be merciful to me: for my soul trusts in you: yes, in the shadow of your wings will I make my refuge, until these calamities be over."*

Another one of these translation errors is written about next.

Christiaan J. de Ruiter

## 3 BACKGROUND OF THE TALLIT

One of these translational errors is written in *Matthew 6 : 6 "But thou, when thou prayest, enter into thy closet (g5009) and when thou hast shut thy door, pray to thy Father which is in secret; and thy Father which seeth in secret shall reward thee openly."*

The Greek word for closet is tamieion [tam-i'-on] a dispensary or magazine, i.e. a chamber on the ground-floor (generally used for storage or privacy, a spot for retirement):
--secret chamber, closet, storehouse. Enter into your tamieion: your chamber, your secret, quiet spot, your closet.

The Hebrew word is h2647 chuppah coming from chaphah h2645 meaning a canopy,chamber, closet, or defense. From which again is derived the cloak or garment of the tallit: A square cover like the chuppah. Enter into your tallit, used  in the old testament writings as the secret room, the Holy of Holies, enclose yourself and pray.

The Jews, which also means Jesus, understood the idea of a mobile tabernacle, outer court, inner court and an Holy of Holies. When the Jews were in the wilderness, they understood the meaning of the tabernacle. With so many of them, they took a little tent, Tallit, and covered themselves thus separating themselves from the world. So when you pray, wrap yourself in your closet, in your tallit and separate yourself from the world.

The disciples also had a solid understanding of this as well. Jesus said that we are taking this from the old covenant and into the new covenant. When you pray, wrap yourself into your prayer closet:your tallit.
Now the question is, what is so special about this chuppah with tassels?

"TALLIT (Heb. TyZt, pl. tallitot; Yid. tales, pl. talesim), prayer shawl. Originally the word meant "gown" or "cloak." This was a rectangular mantle that looked like a blanket and was worn by men in ancient times. At the four corners of the tallit tassels were attached in fulfillment of the biblical commandment of tzitzit (Encyclopedia Judaica)

The importance and special meaning is all in the commandment of tzitzit in;

*Numbers 15:37-41 "And the LORD spake unto Moses, saying, Speak unto the children of Israel, and bid them that they make them fringes (tzitziot) in the borders of their garments throughout their generations, and that they put upon the fringe of the borders a ribband of blue: And it shall be unto you for a fringe, that ye may look upon it, and remember all the commandments of the LORD, and do them ; and that ye seek not after your own heart and your own eyes, after which ye use to go a whoring: That ye may remember, and do all my commandments, and be holy unto your God. I am the LORD your God, which brought you out of the land of Egypt, to be your God: I am the LORD your God."*

## Why?

"because I am the Lord your God
who brought you out of Egypt to be your God.."

The tallit was usually made either of wool or of linen and probably resembled the abbayah ("blanket") still worn by Bedouin for protection against the weather. The tallit made of finer quality was similar to the Roman pallium and was worn mostly by the wealthy and by distinguished rabbis and scholars. The length of the mantle was to be a handbreadth shorter than that of the garment underneath it. After the exile of the Jews from Erez Israel and their dispersion, they came to adopt the fashions of their gentile neighbors more readily.

The tallit was discarded as a daily habit and it became a religious garment for prayer; hence its later meaning of prayer shawl. The tallit was usually white and made either of wool, cotton, or silk, although Maimonides and Alfasi objected to the use of the latter. Strictly observant Jews preferred tallit made of coarse half-bleached lamb's wool. In remembrance of the blue thread of the tzitzit, most talliot have several blue stripes woven into the white material. Until recently, however, they only had black stripes.

## What Is A Tallit (Plural: Talliot)?

Meaning of the Prayer-Shawl: It is a garment made of one piece of material worn around the shoulders.

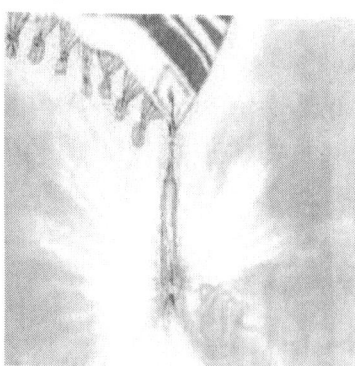

## What Is A Tzitzit? (Plural: Tzitziot)

Also called gadilim (twisted tassel with a knot)
It is a lock, a fringe, a tassel, or forelock of hair.

## Where is it in Scripture?

*Deuteronomy 22:12 "You shall make tassels on the four corners of your garment with which you cover yourself."*

# 4 GEMATRIA OF THE TALLIT

In the tallit, there is a lot of teaching. The teaching of the numbers, called Gematria (Hebrew), is the knowledge about numerical values.

Each word and number have numerical values. (numerology).

These tzitziot are attached to the four corners of the tallit the prayer shawl, the Little Tent. This was what Jesus referred to when he said;

*Matthew 6 : 6 "But you, when you pray, enter into your closet, and when you have shut your door, pray to your Father which is in secret; and your Father which sees in secret shall reward you openly."*

By wrapping yourself in the tallit, this way creating an individual little tent, you separate yourself from the world and are surrounded by God and His commandments.

The tzitzit on each of the four corners has a special meaning. To start our quest into understanding, we need to know that in the Hebrew language we do not have separate characters for numbers. However, the characters do represent numbers at the same time called the Gematria.

Tzitzit need to be kosher and for that they need to be made by a rabbi. Paul, a little tent maker, was one of those rabbi. Paul's very rich friend, Lydia provided him with the die for the tekhelet (the blue string in the tzitzit).

When Jesus said to go into your prayer closet, he did not say to do away with the tallit, but to use it properly. So let's have a look at the tzitzit itself and why an important person like Paul was involved in making them.

## Gematria

The tzitzit was created out of 3 white threads and 1 royal blue thread (the Techelet), folded thus making 8 strings.

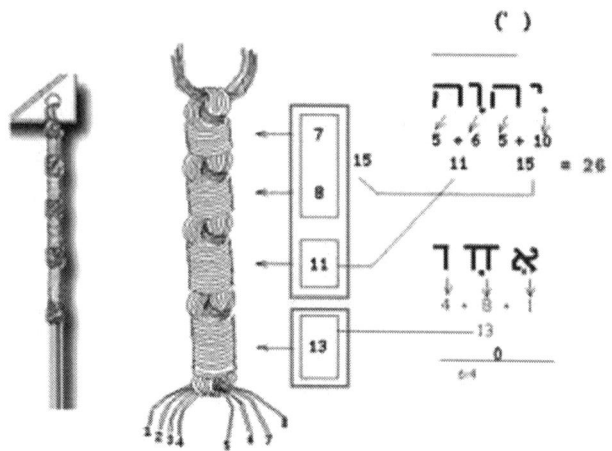

Every corner of the Tallit would have a Tzitzit. This way the wearer would remember God YHVH(Yahweh) and His commandments. The Tzitzit faced in every direction, North, East, South, West.

These 8 strings are tied in the following ways:
- 5 knots with windings in-between
- the First knot, followed by 7 windings
- the Second knot, followed by 8 windings
- the Third knot, followed by 11 windings
- the Fourth knot, followed by 13 windings
- closed with the Fifth knot.

In Hebrew, there are not any tokens for numbers; letters are also numbers.

When looking at the tzitzit we are reminded about the following;

- 7 – 8 – 11 stands in Hebrew for YHVH. (Yahweh) Yod Hey Vav Hey
- 13 stands for echad meaning one or is one. Therefore the windings of each Tzitzit equals the value of YHWH Echad (Jehovah God is One) Which makes God one in unity or Jehovah God is One. This is called the "Shemah" in Hebrew on which the Jewish faith is built.
- Each Tzitzit has 7 white strands (number of perfection) surrounded by the blue servant or "shamash" (color of royalty) Shamash is also the center or middle candle of the menorah (a symbol for Yeshuah, the Servant of God, the Mediator, who stands between the Father and us).
- This now adds up to 8, which is the number of new beginnings.

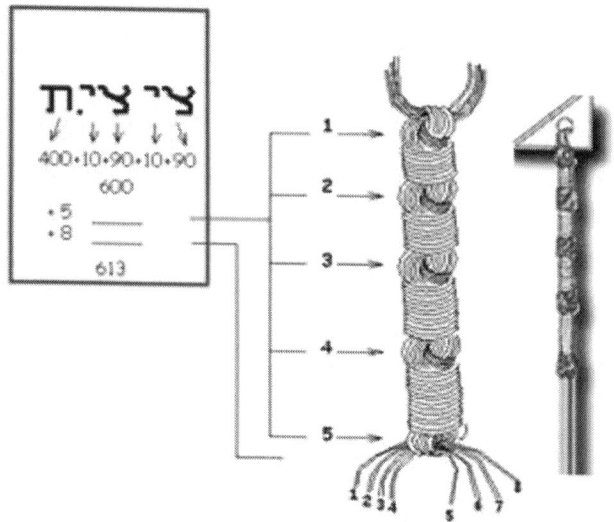

The 8 strings on each of the 4 corners makes 32 which represent the word for heart which makes it to represent God's heart strings.

The 5 knots represent the word of God, the Torah.

The word Tzitzit is spelled;

Tsade Yod Tsade Yod Tav which is in the Gematria 90 + 10 + 90 + 10 + 400 thus equaling 600. Adding the value of the Tzitzit which is 600 to the 5 knots and 8 strands, you have 613. This is the number of mitzvahs, commandments and Blessings of the Tenach (Old Testament) This represents the Word of God. In biblical times, believers wore this all the time as a symbol to be surrounded by the Word of God and by the Presence of God.

Numbers 15:40 *"said so that you should remember all the commandments of the Lord"*

Power in His Wings

There are 613 commandments: 365 Thou shall not and 248 Thou shall commandments.

The number 248 is also the number of significant bones and organs in the human body, while 365 is believed to be the number of ligaments in the human body. God was certainly not just talking to the Jews with the Tzitzit.

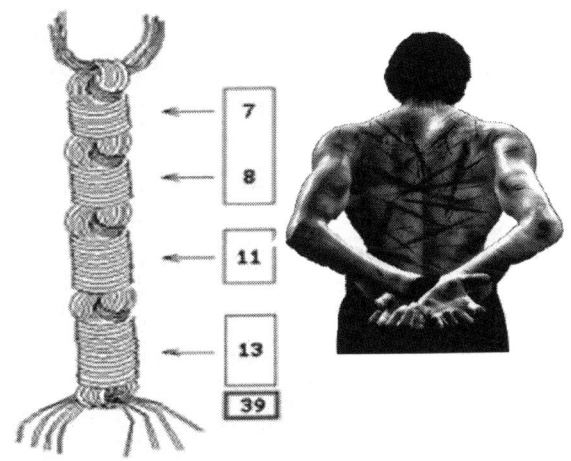

Each tassel (Tzitzit) should have 39 windings (7+8+11+13) they are separated by double knots. The numerical value of YHWH is 26.

Jesus suffered the same number of stripes, 39, for our healing in Isaiah 53:5 also repeated in
1 Peter 2:24.

*Isaiah 53:5 "But he was wounded for our transgressions, he was bruised for our iniquities: the chastisement of our peace was upon him; and with his stripes we are healed."*

*1 Peter 2:24 "Who his own self bare our sins in his own body on the tree, that we, being dead to sins, should live unto righteousness: by whose stripes ye were healed. "*

Jesus received 39 lashes, and by His stripes, we are healed.

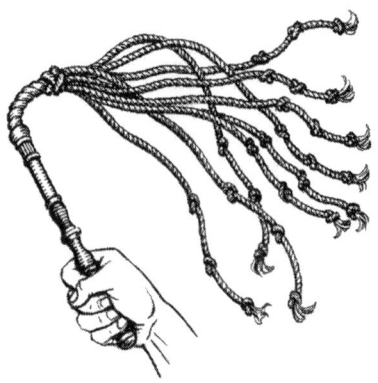

Scripture does not exactly tell how many lashes Jesus Christ received; however, the Roman customary punishment would consist out of 40 lashes with a cat of nine tails, minus one.

As the apostle Paul tells us in *2 Corinthians 11:24* *"Of the Jews five times received I forty stripes save one."*

The blue techelet thread reminds the wearer that they are royalty, the sons of God. This blue thread also reminds of life, the blue air, the blue water of the see, the water of life, given by God's royalty Jesus Christ, and blue from the throne of God.

# 5 WEARING THE TALLIT

Why would we be wanting to wear a tallit? One wears a tallit in order to be surrounded by the Word and the presence of God through the symbols of the Prayer-Shawl.
The Meaning Of Tallit: TALL is the Hebrew word for tent and IT is little
The Literal meaning is therefore " little tent". Paul, coming from rabbinical background, was not making a living from making camping tents. He was very intelligent and studied the Torah. Paul's understanding of the meaning of each thread of the garment made him a better tallit maker.

*Acts 18:2-3 "And found a certain Jew named Aquila, born in Pontus, lately come from Italy, with his wife Priscilla; (because that Claudius had commanded all Jews to depart from Rome:) and came unto them. And because he was of the same craft, he abode with them, and wrought: for by their occupation they were tentmakers."*

Aquila and Priscilla had the same profession and could teach others. They were believing Jews that were persecuted in Rome for faith in Yeshuah.

A tallit is a garment used in prayer symbolizing (prophetically) embraced in the Spirit of God. It means to be physically, spiritually, emotionally covered by God our Adonai (our Lord).

It is a covering. A tallit is a prayer closet to experience the glory of the Lord when you are alone with Him. It is then put over the head to be free from worldly influences and concentrate on Him.

## When Was It Used?

Believers in the Old Testament wore it all the time during prayer. It was specially used at major festivals, funerals and major ceremonies:

- Succoth (Feast of Tabernacles),
- Shavuot (Pentecost),
- Pesach (Easter),
- Yom Kippur (Day of atonement)
- Schacharit (Morning Service) etc.

## The Tallit Symbolizes:

1. The brooding of God's Spirit over the waters in *Genesis 1:2 "And the earth was without form, and void; and darkness was upon the face of the deep. And the Spirit of God moved upon the face of the waters."*
2. The spreading of the wings of eagles in *Deuteronomy 32:1 "As an eagle stirreth up her nest, fluttereth over her young, spreadeth abroad her wings, taketh them, beareth them on her wings" Isaiah 40:31 "But they that wait upon the LORD shall renew their strength; they shall mount up with wings as eagles; they shall run, and not be weary; and they shall walk, and not faint."*
3. Overshadowing of Most High (Holy Spirit) conception of Yeshuah in *Luke 1:35 "And the angel answered and said unto her, The Holy Ghost shall come upon thee, and the power of the Highest shall overshadow thee: therefore also that holy thing which shall be born of thee shall be called the Son of God."* .
4. Shadow of God's wings in *Psalm 36:7 "How excellent is thy loving kindness, O God! therefore the children of men put their trust under the shadow of thy wings."*
5. The passing of the prophetic mantle from Elijah to Elisha In *2 Kings 2:13-14 "He took up also the mantle of Elijah that fell from him, and went back, and stood by the bank of Jordan; And he took the mantle of Elijah that fell from him, and smote the waters, and said, Where is the LORD God of Elijah? and when he also had smitten the*

waters, they parted hither and thither: and Elisha went over."
6. The healing of the woman with the issue of blood *Luke 8:43-48* "And a woman having an issue of blood twelve years, which had spent all her living upon physicians, neither could be healed of any, Came behind him, and touched the border of his garment: and immediately her issue of blood stanched. And Jesus said, Who touched me? When all denied, Peter and they that were with him said, Master, the multitude throng thee and press thee, and sayest thou, Who touched me? And Jesus said, Somebody hath touched me: for I perceive that virtue is gone out of me. And when the woman saw that she was not hid, she came trembling, and falling down before him, she declared unto him before all the people for what cause she had touched him, and how she was healed immediately. And he said unto her, Daughter, be of good comfort: thy faith hath made thee whole; go in peace."
7. Raising the dead *Mark 5:41* "And he took the damsel by the hand, and said unto her, Talitha cumi; which is, being interpreted, Damsel, I say unto thee, arise."
(tallit=covering; cumi=rise up).
8. Declaration that faith is for all nations. Jews and Gentiles alike. *Acts 10:9-11* "On the morrow, as they went on their journey, and drew nigh unto the city, Peter went up upon the housetop to pray about the sixth hour: And he became very hungry, and would have eaten: but while they made ready, he fell into a trance, And saw heaven

*opened, and a certain vessel descending upon him, as it had been a great sheet knit at the four corners, and let down to the earth:"* This cloth is a tallit. This means "He now can go and bring the Word to the Gentiles". Note: Peter never ate the unclean animals. The vision of the tallit meant all nations are accepted by faith in Yeshuah and no-one is unclean that follows the Lord. Peter got the message to not only teach Jews but also Gentiles.

9. *Revelation 19:13-16 "And he was clothed with a vesture dipped in blood: and his name is called The Word of God. And the armies which were in heaven followed him upon white horses, clothed in fine linen, white and clean. And out of his mouth goeth a sharp sword, that with it he should smite the nations: and he shall rule them with a rod of iron: and he treadeth the winepress of the fierceness and wrath of Almighty God. And he hath on his vesture and on his thigh a name written, KING OF KINGS, AND LORD OF LORDS."* Tallit dipped in blood is the Word of God the robe Jesus wore had YHWH Echad on it meaning King of Kings and Lord of Lords. What kind of robe would our returning Yeshuah wear?

10. Peter went into the empty tomb and found the tallit of Jesus. *John 20:6-7 "Then cometh Simon Peter following him, and went into the sepulchre, and seeth the linen clothes lie, And the napkin, that was about his head, not lying with the linen clothes, but wrapped together in a place by itself.* (a symbol of the Resurrection)

11. A covenant sign Ruth 3:9 "spread your tallit over me" During a Jewish wedding (called ketubah) the bride and groom are covered with the "chupah" a canopy which is a large tallit. It is held by friends over the couple by the four corners (Tzitzit) . We read in the Bible that in the last days, goyim (gentiles) will cling to the Tzitzit of one Jew.
12. Matthew.14:36. The sick begged Him that they might only touch the Tzitzit of His garment. Each person thattouched it were made perfectly well.
13. In Revelations 4:8 we see the four living creatures with six wings who cry: "Holy, holy, holy." They surround the throne of God in the temple. Are we not the temple of the Holy Spirit of God? The Jewish flag is like a tallit: white and blue. If you put the Magen David in the middle (shield of David or Jewish star) than it is. (Could this be a symbol for the Morning star too? The devil lost that title in Isaiah 14:12 and Yeshuah is the Morning star Revelation 22:16) To me, personally it is just the Jewish flag.

# Jesus Is The Lily Of The Valley And The Bright And Morning star!!

# Power in His Wings

In the book of Numbers, Balaam had to curse Israel and could not.
*Numbers 24:5 "How goodly are thy tents, O Jacob, and thy tabernacles, O Israel!"*
he said. All believers had the tallit over them in the desert making one big tabernacle. In the wilderness, Moses set up a tent (tabernacle) of meeting according to the command of God. Two and a half million Jewish people could not have pitched a tent on desert sand. They were together each in their little tent. A protection from harm.

As the tallit is placed over the head, it forms a tent with the four Tzitzit on each corner. The word for corners in Hebrew is kanaph. This also means wings. It is the same word used for the wings of the Seraphim in *Isaiah 6:2 Above it stood the seraphims: each one had six wings; with twain he covered his face, and with twain he covered his feet, and with twain he did fly.*

As your arms are held out under the garment, wings are formed and each corner is a kanaph or wing.

Christiaan J. de Ruiter

# 6 TALLIT SCRIPTURES

Other Scriptures Mentioned In Connection With The Tallit:

*Psalm 36:7 "How excellent is thy loving kindness, O God! therefore the children of men put their trust under the shadow of thy wings."*

*Malachi 4:2 "But unto you that fear my name shall the Sun of righteousness arise with healing in his wings; and ye shall go forth, and grow up as calves of the stall."*

*Psalm 84:1 "How amiable are thy tabernacles, O LORD of hosts!"*

*Psalm 61:4 "I will abide in thy tabernacle for ever: I will trust in the covert of thy wings. Selah."*

*Psalm 27:5-6 "For in the time of trouble he shall hide me in his pavilion: in the secret of his tabernacle shall he hide me; he shall set me up upon a rock. And now shall mine head be lifted up above mine enemies round about me: therefore will I offer in his tabernacle sacrifices of joy; I will sing, yea, I will sing praises unto the LORD."*

In *Ezekiel 16:8*: the Lord speaks to Jerusalem: *"Now when I passed by thee, and looked upon thee, behold, thy time was the time of love; and I spread my (tallit) skirt over thee (kanaph), and covered thy nakedness: yea, I sware unto thee, and entered into a covenant with thee, saith the Lord GOD, and thou becamest mine."*
In Psalm 91: we are able to abide "under the shadow of the Almighty" - and "under His wings."
*Psalm 91:1,4 "1 He that dwelleth in the secret place of the most High shall abide under the shadow of the Almighty. 4 He shall cover thee with his feathers, and under his wings shalt thou trust: his truth shall be thy shield and buckler. "*

Could there be a connection with the revival in England when Susanna Wesley prayed for her nation with a garment over her head? Her prayers changed the history of England.
There is power in the Name of Jesus. We may use our hands, feet and even clothes to help pray for revival in our homes, families and nations.

# 7 HOW TO WEAR THE TALLIT

Wear it around your shoulders as you worship the Lord and intercede if you like. You can also wear it over your head. Some orthodox rabbis say that it is mandatory for a man to wear a tallit and it is optional for women. Do not let this stop you as a woman of God from entering into its blessing by wearing it.
***Galatians 3:28*** *"There is neither Jew nor Greek, there is neither bond nor free, there is neither male nor female: for ye are all one in Christ Jesus."*

We are one in Christ Jesus. This is an antidote against inferiority. Use it prophetically.

Christiaan J. de Ruiter

# Lettering On The Tallit:

This is called the "atarah", the band on the top of the garment. It is called the crown of the garment. It is the blessing:

Barukh atah Adonai, Eloheinu, melekh ha'olam asher kidishanu b'mitz'votav v'tzivanu l'hit'ateif ba-tzitzit

בָּרוּךְ אַתָּה יְיָ אֱלֹהֵינוּ מֶלֶךְ הָעוֹלָם
אֲשֶׁר קִדְּשָׁנוּ בְּמִצְוֹתָיו וְצִוָּנוּ
לְהִתְעַטֵּף בַּצִּיצִית

"Blessed art Thou, Lord our God, King of the Universe, Who has sanctified us with His commandments and commanded us to wrap ourselves in the Tzitzit."
The lettering is always on the outside just like the tent walls of the Holy Tabernacle so that they would always hang the same way.

# 8 RELIGIOSITY OF THE TALLIT

## Is It Religious To Wear A Tallit And Is It Necessary?

No, it is not necessary at all and it is not religious either. It is, however, in the Bible. God is teaching us through the natural Israel what it means to be in the Spirit of understanding for His Word. It teaches us to love the Bible and the Jewish background of the Word so we will not be tempted to be anti-Semitic. We will be ready for the End-time Plan and will be able to teach the Jewish people about their own Bible through the Spirit of Jesus.

It is a wonderful experience to know that you are under the wings of God almighty, holding on to the tzitzit, the name of God, the promise of Jesus, the commandments and promises of the Heavenly father.

Being covered by His love, under His firmament, inside of your own personal tabernacle, prayer closet, secret place, just you and God.

Do you need covering today? Do you need healing? Do you need the love of the Almighty and the miracle

power in your situation?
Come. For He is the God that healeth Thee. He is the Lord your Healer. Jehovah Raphah.

# Appendice
# A. Scripture and key words

1 Peter 2:24 ..................................................... 19

2 Corinthians 11:24 ........................................ 20

2 Kings 2:13-14 .............................................. 23

abbayah ........................................................ 13

Acts 10:9-11 ................................................... 24

Acts 18:2-3 ..................................................... 22

Adonai ..................................................... 22, 32

atarah ........................................................... 32

chupah .......................................................... 26

chuppah ........................................................ 12

cumi .............................................................. 24

Deuteronomy 22:12 ...................................... 14

Deuteronomy 32:1 ........................................ 23

echad ............................................................ 17

Echad ...................................................... 17, 25

Ezekiel 16:8 ................................................... 30

| | |
|---|---|
| g5009 | 11 |
| gadilim | 14 |
| Galatians 3:28 | 31 |
| Gematria | 15p., 18 |
| Genesis 1:2 | 23 |
| h2645 | 12 |
| h2647 | 12 |
| Isaiah 14:12 | 26 |
| Isaiah 40:31 | 23 |
| Isaiah 53:5 | 19 |
| Isaiah 6:2 | 27 |
| Jehovah | 17, 34 |
| John 20:6-7 | 25 |
| kanaph | 27, 30 |
| ketubah | 26 |
| Luke 1:35 | 23 |
| Luke 8:43-48 | 24 |
| Magen | 26 |
| Malachi 4:2 | 29 |

| | |
|---|---|
| Mark 5:41 | 24 |
| Matthew 6 : 6 | 11, 15 |
| Matthew.14:36 | 26 |
| menorah | 17 |
| mitzvahs, | 18 |
| Numbers 15:37-41 | 13 |
| Numbers 15:40 | 18 |
| Numbers 24:5 | 27 |
| Pesach | 22 |
| prayer closet | 12, 16, 22, 33 |
| Psalm 27:5-6 | 29 |
| Psalm 36:7 | 23, 29 |
| Psalm 61:4 | 29 |
| Psalm 84:1 | 29 |
| Psalm 91 | 30 |
| Psalm 91:1,4 | 30 |
| Revelation 19:13-16 | 25 |
| Revelation 22:16 | 26 |
| Revelations 4:8 | 26 |

Ruth 3:9 .................................................. 26
Schacharit .................................................. 22
Shamash .................................................. 17
Shavuot .................................................. 22
Shemah .................................................. 17
Succoth .................................................. **22**
talesim .................................................. 13
Talitha cumi .................................................. 24
talli .................................................. 14
talliot .................................................. 14
Talliot .................................................. 14
tallit .................................. 12pp., 21p., 24pp., 30p.
Tallit .................. i, v, 14, 17, 21, 23, 25, 29, 32p.
TALLIT .................................................. 13
tallitot .................................................. 13
techelet .................................................. 20
Techelet .................................................. 16
tekhelet .................................................. 16
Tenach .................................................. 18

Torah..................18, 21

tzitziot..................13, 15

Tzitziot..................14

tzitzit..................13p., 16p., 32p.

Tzitzit..................14, 16pp., 26p., 32

Yahweh..................17

Yeshuah..................**17,** 22p., 25p.

YHVH..................17

YHVH(Yahweh)..................17

YHWH..................17, 25

YHWH is 26..................19

Yom Kippur..................22

Christiaan J. de Ruiter

# B. HEBREW – ENGLISH

| | |
|---|---|
| Abbayah | Woolen Blanket worn by Bedouins |
| Adonai | Lord |
| Atarah | Crown or Head band |
| Chupah, Chuppah, Chaphah | Canopy |
| Cumi | Rise up |
| Echad | One, or is One |
| Gadilim | Twisted tassel with a knot |
| Gematria | Knowledge about letter values in Hebrew, but this is NOT numerology |
| Ha'Mashiah | The Messiah, or the Deliverer |
| Kanaph | Corner or Wings |
| Ketubah | Marriage Contract |
| Magen | Shield or Star |
| Menorah | 7 Arm Candle holder |
| Mitzvahs | Commandments |
| Pesach | Passover |

| | |
|---|---|
| Rapha | Healer |
| Schacharit | Morning Service |
| Shamash | Servant |
| Shavuot | Pentecost |
| Shema, Shema, sh'ma | Hear |
| Succoth | Feast of the Tabernacles |
| Talesim | See Talliot |
| Talitha cumi | Little Girl rise up, or come from under the Tallit |
| Talliot, tallitot | Plural of Tallit |
| Tallit | Prayer-Shawl |
| Techelet, Tekhelet | The Servant string |
| Tenach, Tanakh | Old Testament |
| Torah | The Law, first 5 books of the Bible |
| Tzitziot | Plural of Tzitzit |
| Tzitzit | Tassel, see Gadilim |
| Yahweh, YHVH, YHWH, Jehovah | God |
| Yeshuah | Jesus |
| Yom Kippur | Day of attonement |

# C. STRONGS REFERENCES

G5009
class="greek"ταμεῖον akin to τέμνω, to cut); a dispensary or magazine, i.e. a chamber on the ground-floor or interior of an Oriental house (generally used for storage or privacy, a spot for retirement)
Derivation: neuter contraction of a presumed derivative of ταμίας (a dispenser or distributor;
KJV Usage: secret chamber, closet, storehouse.
Thayer:
1) a storage chamber, storeroom
2) a chamber esp. an inner chamber
3) a secret room
Vine's Expository Dictionary of New Testament Words
ταμεῖον
tameion
*tam-i'-on*
Neuter contraction of a presumed derivative of ταμίας tamias (a *dispenser* or *distributor,* akin to

τέμνω temnō , to cut); a *dispensary* or *magazine*, that is, a chamber on the ground floor or interior of an Oriental house (generally used for *storage* or *privacy*, a spot for retirement)
KJV Usage: secret chamber, closet, storehouse.

## H2645
חפה
châphâh
khaw-faw'
A primitive root; to cover; by implication to veil, to incase, protect
KJV Usage: ceil, cover, overlay.
חפה
1. to cover, overlay, wainscotted, covered with boards or panelling
a. (Qal) to cover
b. (Niphal) to be covered
c. (Piel) to cover, overlay
Origin: a primitive root
Parts of Speech: Verb

## H2647
חפה
chûppâh
khoop-paw'
The same as; Chuppah, an Israelite
KJV Usage: Huppah.
חפה
Huppah = "canopy"
1. a priest of the 13th course in the time of David
Parts of Speech: Proper Name Masculine

# ABOUT THE AUTHOR

Dr. Christiaan J. de Ruiter was born in the Netherlands as the youngest of six children. He grew up going to church in the Salvation Army and became involved in the choir and brass band. After his move to the United States of America, he has been involved in the American branch of the Salvation Army as a local officer, bandmaster (conductor) and instructor. While involved in the Salvation Army, many ministry trips have been made throughout the western US, spreading the gospel through word and song. Still there was more for him to explore and Christiaan accepted a position as associate pastor in the Free Will Baptist church. However short lived, this was a great time of learning. His dear friend Dr. J.B. Davidson finally placed the question in his heart; Isn't it time to make a true decision for Christ and pastor the church, which calling is upon your life? Christiaan took this word of God and prayed about it. New Beginnings Christian Center was given birth by the two friends and provided much needed ministry in prayer and healing in Murray, Utah. Family circumstances made it necessary to dissolve this ministry while moving to Texas in 2007. After a period of personal struggle and growth, a small church was born and an affiliation grew out of it. This was the start of Eagle Wings Charismatic Ministries International.

Learn more about this ministry at www.ewcmi.us and become part of this by giving some of your time or by becoming a partner by your financial giving.

Made in the USA
San Bernardino, CA
18 March 2016